THE
NEW SHORTER
OXFORD ENGLISH
DICTIONARY

THE
NEW SHORTER
OXFORD ENGLISH
DICTIONARY

ON HISTORICAL PRINCIPLES

EDITED BY

LESLEY BROWN

VOLUME 2

N–Z

Oxford University Press, Walton Street, Oxford OX2 6DP

Oxford New York Toronto
Delhi Bombay Calcutta Madras Karachi
Kuala Lumpur Singapore Hong Kong Tokyo
Nairobi Dar es Salaam Cape Town
Melbourne Auckland Madrid
and associated companies in
Berlin Ibadan

Oxford is a trade mark of Oxford University Press

Published in the United States by
Oxford University Press Inc., New York

First Edition 1933
Second Edition 1936
Third Edition 1944
Reprinted with Revised Etymologies and Enlarged Addenda 1973
This Edition 1993
Reprinted (with corrections) 1993

British Library Cataloguing in Publication Data
Data available

Library of Congress Cataloging in Publication Data
Data available

ISBN 0-19-861134-X Plain Edition
ISBN 0-19-861271-0 Thumb Index Edition
ISBN 0-19-195804-2 Leather Bound Edition

3 5 7 9 10 8 6 4 2

Text processed by Oxford University Press
Typeset in Monotype Plantin by
Barbers Ltd., Wrotham, Kent
Printed in the United States of America
on acid-free paper